KNOCK KNOCK

KNOCK KNOCK

Heather Hartley

CARNEGIE MELLON UNIVERSITY PRESS
PITTSBURGH 2010

Acknowledgments

The author and publisher acknowledge, with gratitude, the following publications in which these poems first appeared:

Antietam Review: "Epilogue in a City Garden"
CALYX: "Nudes in a New England Barn"
Drunken Boat: "Advice for the Hirsute," "Director of the Feast," "Pledge"
Forklift, Ohio: "Artichoke Horoscope"
Kalliope: "The Bibliothèque nationale"
The Los Angeles Review: "The Sorceress of the Russian Sauna"
96 Inc.: "Postscript by a Park Bench"
Mississippi Review: "Full Pleather Moon"
Paris/Atlantic (France): "Epilogue in a City Garden," "Nudes in a New England Barn"
Pharos (France): "Rhapsody in Blue in Front of a Statue of Alexander Pushkin"
POOL: "The *Prix-fixe* in Petersburg"
Post Road: "The Karma Club," "Partner, my partner"
Saint Petersburg Review: "The Madonnas of Montepertuso"
Smartish Pace: "The Flying Machine, or Elegy for the Twentieth Century"
Threshold: Passages from Prague: "Rhapsody in Blue in Front of a Statue of Alexander Pushkin"
Tin House: "Elegy in India Ink," "The Seventh Art in the Sanatorium"
Upstairs at Duroc (France): "Broad Strokes in a Wine Bar," "In a Train Tunnel"
Zócalo Press (England): "Elegy for Napoli," "To My One Love's Letter"

"Elegy in India Ink" appears in the anthology *Satellite Convulsions: Poems from Tin House*. "Epithalamium," "Rapunzel on an Ironing Board," "Sweet Woodruff," and "To My One Love's Letter" appear on the Dorothy Sargent Rosenberg website, http://www.dorothyprizes.org/. "Postscript by a Park Bench" also appears in *A Time of Trial, Beyond the Terror of 9/11*.

Book design: Rachael Clemmons

The publication of this book is made possible by a grant from the Pennsylvania Council on the Arts.

Library of Congress Control Number 2009930164
ISBN 978-0-88748-519-0

10 9 8 7 6 5 4 3 2 1

PENNSYLVANIA
COUNCIL
ON THE

ARTS

For my mother and father

Contents

V

I

This is a fugue for the lost art of aching.

This is a place where all the keepsakes are sleeping.
Be ready.
Have a pastoral disregard for the taste of it all.
Mix the sweet and sour with jealousy.
Mix without hope, mix barbarically.
Because all the angels are out to lunch and send their regrets.
Because that's what the family recipe calls for
and you must follow it.
Choices are left at the door by the duck shoes and pitchforks.
When you are old enough,
put all of this abandonment in a stew.
Make music, sit on a stranger's lap and serve.

Artichoke Horoscope

Vegetables are a catalyst this month—
and the elected legume is the artichoke!
A tenacious vegetable, gruff on the outside,
leafy, tricky, not inelegant
and with the sweetest, most desirable interior—
like you.

Let your partner know you're not won over
like any old easy green bean—
ten minutes of careless boiling and *basta*.
It takes time and careful attention
to pluck, savor and suck out
your breathtaking core.

This month, your star-crossed moon
is in the casserole.

The Karma Club

—at a poetry reading

Around the room, merry-go-round,
you find Mr. Desmond, the tax collector

writing villanelles, his head a hurricane
of baldness, sucking on the stub of a cigarette.

Next to him, a convention of Barbie dolls in black Tencel pants
followed by scant PhDs scouting their own knot

with a nod to patrons, of course, dull in thick gold
and polyeser blends, older than Ganesh.

The shrine of the bar floats in the foggy distance,
beatitude passes by on a bamboo tray

and smiling with salsa between my teeth,
I persevere in my quest—

to search for the face that will reveal my fate in a wine glass,
on a paper napkin, let slip between beer nuts

my being and nothingness, who will pull out
from beneath me a rabbit, a rubber duck,

disclose the future in my fingertips and bra straps,
who from behind my ear will pull out a silver ducat.

Knock Knock

His fork outlasted his fuck.

His landlord was the king of butter.

His confidant the local barber.

He had a bitchy page.

Drank bitter bitters.

Knew a Senator who couldn't masticate.

Saw Padua from a pension.

Sérénissime.

There's a powdered wig and a mask involved.

A wayward monk and a wooden spoon.

An amazon in an auberge.

Macaroni, clitoris, ink.

A dictionary of cheese.

Candle wax and dead skin.

Flacons and tinctures and blancmange.

A singular gondola.

The Cabbala.

A woman with yellow roses in her gloved hands.

Someone's at the servant's door, someone's at the *porte cochère*.

Knock knock.

Who's there?

Casanova.

Full Pleather Moon

A thin East Indian man in a baby blue suit with a toilet seat on his lap looks up at the subway map. Dark hands knuckle the sides and oval brown fingernails are rimmed with dirt. Squirming the slightest bit, the man stares ahead. A pencil-thin moustache and cracked tan lips drop down to a chinless chin. He has caught me looking at him, looking as if I wondered where he might be going with *that* in his possession. All of a sudden, I have to pee. *Now.* He blinks at me worriedly and hugs the seat closer to his chest. The half moons of his thumbs grip its sloping sides. He holds his breath. The subway slows, he turns away, it stops, he stands, grasps the portable loo as the doors open and then, flushed, takes his full pleather moon onto the next stop.

Drip

Here comes my hostess naked with a wrench—
you could say it was Max's fault, Max, with a capital *M*—
it's his place on the *gracht*, his sounds in the night—
but between himself in Madrid and himself in that Italian villa,

we're back to the configuration of Nikki and me,
an art deco mirror, a marble bathroom,
and Amsterdam in November—
but this is all anecdotal.

Cometh my mistress bared, wraunch-wristed,
laurels in hair, she launches, forte and foretold,
into Maximilian's error with much ado—
Maximilian, with an upper-case *M*,
traipsing through the *gracht* at crepuscule
nick nick nick

All I was trying to do was wash my hair
in an apartment only an Andalusian woman could love—
you could say that was Max's fault—
his vegetable love for antique brass—

But I'm still thinking about her breasts—
how they looked like mine, but thirty years older,
lighter in color, same shape,
band aids, mirror, mirror.

This is my mistress of the housetess,
with the mostess, with the bustiness of a mousetess,
with four breasts between us and some ice water,
let me introduce you to myself, then—
later, older, saggier, and I think, most happier.

Nudes in a New England Barn

Suddenly, the barn fills with nudes.
They pour through the double wooden door, drop down from the hay-
loft, climb through windows—pink impasto figures, fine fresco thin
limbs, a baker's dozen of breasts, rolls of pale green flesh or skin taught
as stretched canvas, rough and white to touch. Models thick as thieves
everywhere you look.

Ingres, stamping mud clots from his boots, ushers in two serpent-armed women,
twins, in turbans and with pale skin.
Rubens' shy wife twists impossibly around herself, cornered in a fur
wrap. Delacroix's tormented women fall off of Shaker chairs, backs
arched, onto the barn wood floor. A titter rises in the room as bloody
bloody Bacon drops some screaming scraps at the door. Four models
of Modigliani enter from the left, hands linked, silent, proud, self-
absorbed. They carry their flat beauty with them as if on a frieze.

In the back of the barn, Jane Avril adjusts her stockings.
The three flaunting graces are there, La Goulue picks straw bits from
her hair. Paris sits in a corner judging. Toulouse-Lautrec's green
whores mill around touching their enormous hair. Elizabeth Siddal
takes another draught of laudanum. Two Austrian girls mutter guttural
swears and curse an absent Egon S., lover and depraved pervert
extraordinaire.

Giacometti, worried, searches for Diego's head among the dung and damp hay.
He's lost the damned metaphorical thing again, and knows he must start

over from scratch—give the poor man another cigarette. Rodin knits his knotty, plaster-crusted hands in his beard, unsure of what to do next.

Balthus watches the whole scene from a corner in a kimono, smoking, in dark glasses. His matte nudes are cast against late afternoon light, a glow of green and red tones. His girls leave a scent of apples in the room. Picasso, snug in the hayloft, strokes his damzelles d'Avignon—he could give two figs. The ladies sleep on, dreaming their Spanish dreams. Italian models, nameless, dot the room with dark parts and loud shouts—you can barely stir them with a stick. Jeanne Hébuterne, Modigliani's wife with the wild and soft grey eyes, throws herself out the window to make more room.

Here, the scent of flesh overpowers any smell of paint, for there is a woman here— behind the door, behind the canvas too—there is one even watching you. For this is the largest retrospective ever—Italian, French, Goddess, Whore, Nude, Model, Little Girl. Death and the Maiden. Wife taking a bath. Young girl with arms crossed tightly across her chest. *La Grande Odalisque.* The painted, not the paintings.

The woman, the real one, unties her sash, steps out of her robe and mounts the platform in the studio. (She's the one praying it will be warm.) (She's the one with aches and pains and sighs, the one with tired eyes.) She leads her still life the whole time the others have been making noise. You may not know her name, but you will want to greet her anyway. She's waiting.

To My One Love's Letter

My darling M—,

The alphabet is anorexic.
There's not enough flesh
to express what I mean—
ABC, TUV.

Suffice it to say
my heart is the verb
you conjugate perfectly.

M marks the spot dark and hot
where I'm under my one
love's letter's spell.

Advice for the Hirsute

I've decided it's not a good excuse—
it could eat you for the rest of your days.

He never calls me bella. 'La mia ragazza,' etc.,
but it's been about three weeks now, or over a month,
depending on how you count—
(sex).

The lawyer has lost her mind but O can she dance.
For years, she didn't like her hands
but you can only hide them so long, I said, *a girl's only got so many pockets.*
(Now she's in love with them like a teenage girl.)

If I gave you the same gift again, wrapped differently,
but the same exact thing,
would you be happy again, a second time?

As kitsch as it sounds and as bad as the coffee is, that's how it goes.
You can only wax your crotch so long before finally, finally,
the hair creeps back like dark widow's weeds.

Now put on your words and go out and play with the other kids.
But whatever you do, for god's sake, don't congregate around
    the toilets.

All year has been November—a little gray, worn out—Demeter in rags.

Yesterday, when she was driving, she said in the smallest voice,
What happened to my nice little life?
It was the most devastating thing.

It's like a cat with a sixth claw—
some things you just have to accept.

II

New Year's in Napoli: Twenty-four Resolutions and Curses

"A sciorta e 'a morta stanno addereto â porta."
"Luck and death stand behind the door."
                        —Neapolitan proverb

1
It's New Years' Eve and there's a scorpion in the bathroom.

2
It's New Years' Eve and I'm wearing a new red thong for good luck.

3
Is it bad luck to eat the salami of a dead man?

4
It's New Years' Eve and there's no hot water in the apartment—
    this is bad luck.

5
Is it bad luck to eat the provolone of a dead man?

6
The poisonous mix of no hot water *and* the scorpion in the bathroom
    is *really* bad luck.

7
Driving along a back road, he screamed *touch your tits!* as he
    touched his balls—
an ancient woman in a black skirt had given us the evil eye.

8
Is it bad luck to brush your teeth with the toothpaste of a dead man?

9
Auguri! Prosperity!

10
If you wear a little masquerade mask on December 31st, it may
  bring good luck.

11
Dancing with a stranger might do it too.

12
In the Grand Hotel Vesuvio, just about anything will bring you good luck.
  In fact, if you can stay there, you don't need any more luck at all.

13
Everyone here is named after a saint—it's supposed to bring good luck.

14
Even to the dead man.

15
The Prosecco bottles thrown out of back street apartment windows on
  New Years' Day bring good luck.

16
So do the fires flickering in garbage bins on the Piazza del Plebiscito.

17
Who would have thought that Alberico, the fruit seller with a pear-
  shaped scab above his lip and eyes in the back of his head could be
  right about the dead man?

18
Is it bad luck to pronounce the name of a dead man?

19
(His name was Luca.)

20
There is a word in Italian that has to do with superstition—
Scaramanzia—it sounds like scarecrow, manic, zits.

21
It means spleen, tradition, godsends.

22
We bought figs and mandarins from Alberico—to cancel out Luca's
death and the scorpion's hex.

23
Is it bad luck to thumb your nose at a graveyard?

24
We did not knock on wood once.

The Cardboard Confidante of the Camorra
—Naples, Italy

"Camorra: a secret society of Naples associated with robbery, blackmail
and murder."

—Encyclopedia Britannica

There's a shrine next to the apartment door—
some cardboard saint propped up
against candles and stems
who stays awake all night in this fork of the city
who spies the secrets of the street
who can't stop the killings.

The Madonnas of Montepertuso
—Italy

Santa Maria delle Grazie di Montepertuso
shellacked on a wall, divine head tilted
towards that baby the size of a thumbnail,
hovers over the old double bed
where we whack back and forth
like a two-backed dark-haired beast.

The other Madonnas nailed
above the bed bend gently over
and encourage us.

We confess all on a worn coverlet
offering ardent visions of a different sort
to the loose mountain queens and their flock—
no time to *Hail Mary*, genuflect
or make the sign of the cross.

Side to side the Madonnas sway
as the bed creaks and scrapes
beneath their holy chins—

among the *whoops* and *aaahs*
the angels moan out to us,
the heavenly host pants

and the swinging convent of Montepertuso
doesn't miss a single acrobatic miracle.

But it is really Our Lady of Montepertuso
who nods a yes, who gives us grace, yes, it *is* good—
yes, 69 is her sacred number too—*Go ahead, God bless.*

Elegy for Napoli

"If all the trash [in Southern Italy] that . . . escapes official inspection was collected in one place, it would form a mountain weighing 14 million tons and rising 47,900 feet."

—Roberto Saviano, *Gomorrah: Italy's Other Mafia*

Dear Parthenope,

The Madonnas are gagging on trash. All over the city and in the provinces too. It's not your fault, you've been gone so long, but I wanted you to know. Because like you, we're drowning. Of course it's not the same—we're not sirens in love with a force like Ulysses. But we're sick with your city, sick in love with it.

Napoli is dying a magnificent death. It's the slow, crumbling death of a dowager—regal, inevitable, civic.

The chronicles have been written—the rotten rotten fruit, rats and stench, dried blood, plastic sacs and the burning, burning—wild dogs having the feast of their lives. How animals celebrate our ignorance.

Whispers of tuberculosis, cholera—rumors and dark things. You know what rumors do to gods and humans.

And then the hush hush.

With the exodus of the sun, the men come out and stand in clumps—tall as piles of garbage. They smoke and talk—don't move—they make bonfires with their cigarettes.

What is the cure?

Ulysses, strapped to the mast, escaped you. That night, after he passed, you drank your words. 36 drops of dew in the sea. 16 days and 17 nights. Neapolis—new city—Napoli—was born. All they could see was a whore.

What is the cure?

You should know that trash is filling our throats. That the gods left the city and locked the door, that the children are running wild. That Napoli curls in on itself, crawls back into the sea—no more damp, breamy dream—

Napoli's forgotten her mother.

Throw this litter, letter, into the sea.

This heart was made for stomping—think twice, yours too.

—between Naples, Italy, the Loire Valley in France, and the American Far West

I

We stole landscapes for hours.

Took pictures with no film in the camera.

Mistook local high school girls for whores.

Drove circles around Ballan-Miré—ghost town with a pretty name.

Listened to the theme song from *A Fistful of Dollars* a thousand times.

Drank our way through the rain in Tours.

Wore black and pretended to be dirty, dirty blondes.

II

Imagine yourself in a Stetson.

Your hands make a lariat around the small of my back.

Lasso me in, ride me long—

I don't know how to locate where we made love on a map.

III

There are many Wests

but there is one in the heart

rough and strange with no borders—

a wild place—

to which no one lays claim

without great tenderness,

without your

—my—

deepest consent.

The Amazing Madame Barba of Montepertuso
—Italy

Madame Barba has chickens
that holler all night
and lots of chin hair.

Madame Barba has a monkey face
and eyebrows scratched like lovers' initials in bark.

Madame Barba has bare feet cracked like a summer sidewalk.

Madame Barba talks on and on in dialect
and really does have a little beard—
it's grey and curly and would be so
easy to pluck with tweezers.

I think I should be calling Madame Barba *Signora.*

Madame Barba's cross-eyed son with a limp and thick lips
shows us the way up to a room on the top of a hill,
in a hole, Montepertuso, mountain hole,
where we will spend the night.

Madame Barba has a house that touches the sky.

Partner, my partner
—Naples, Italy

I

My spaghetti western love, I come to you ragged and leggy
from the spanky suburbs of the East Coast of America,
all bones and heat to meet you in the dark pushy
alleys of your native streets—*edicola*, duchy, *vicolo*.

II

Ride me away in your old Opel horse
to the kingdom of Napoli, Forcella,
to the Devil's Fork, where balcony to balcony
women jabber back and forth stirring endless pots of sauce.

III

Here our duels are horizontal, monumental
in back streets where the law won't step foot anymore—
we spar in the dark on floral bedspreads
with long sweet shootouts at two and three and four.

IV

As your sidekick—for now at least—
we hit towns one by one—Lauro, Nola, Avellino—
names that sound like lace on arms—
but none have the feral, fragile sound of Napoli.

V

It's too late to turn back from this bragging sunset
the one that sets on the *acqua pazza* of our lust—
or at least that sets over the gulf—
and from whatever it is that isn't named between us.

VI

Win over my Wild West and so win a piece of me,
desperately, now somewhere lost in the depths
of your Southern Italy. When you sling your arm
over mine, it is possession.

The Sorceress of the Russian Sauna

"Like the overall banya experience, the idea of beating oneself with
branches and leaves to deep-clean skin is really about striking a balance
between pleasure and pain. This is where the Russian master or
mistress of the sauna is crucial."

—*Time Out Guide, Moscow and Saint Petersburg*

The woman who sweeps dropped branches
sweeps away the leaves in heat,
in nothing but slippers and a toboggan hat, head bent,
sweat dripping, she sweeps away the mafia and bribes,
the grime from underneath the Galernaya arch,
dirty words, dead birds,
breasts swinging, she sweeps and sweeps
with a few twigs falling from her witch's broom,
the naked sorceress missing a front tooth,
beat me clean, babushka, please—I'll do anything—
and pushing back a lock of stringy hair, sweeps up
the well-dressed prostitutes of Nevsky Prospekt
and their impeccable pimps,
and with two or three final thrusts out the door,
cleans the world of dirt for good.

Sleeping with *War and Peace*

I

The bed is not really big enough for all of us.
Prince Vasili, arms akimbo, continues to mock Anna Mihalovna.
(Why *did* he do that for Boris, anyway? Was it his father's devotion or
    something else?)
Old Count Bezuhov has been on his deathbed for days—everyone
    holds their breath.
"But we must sleep sometime."
(That was Anna M. again, butting in when no one asked.)
There's Prince Andrei looking glacial and mumbling about
    some attack—
doesn't he ever let his hair down?
Hippolyte excuses himself—time for his medication again.
The little princess with the downy lip knits away her life.
Nothing ever happened at Bald Hills—until Anatole arrived.
Natasha, Natasha, Natasha.
Could Mademoiselle Bourienne please wipe that monkey grin
    off her face?
We all saw what you did in the garden, you French slut.
The old aunt with cataracts waits for her moment in the lampfaded sun.
There goes Prince V. squeezing elbows again—he's about to hit you up.
It was bound to happen—winking at the footmen—
that terrible, inevitable union: Pierre + Hélène = X.
And Pierre, *le pauvre*, must solve for X.

II

What else could we do but we sit by the samovar and bite our
    collective lip?

III

All those icons and bonbons.
All those young men whose first names end in vowels
and whose haircuts suck.
Hussar, Cossack, gimp.
A huge salver and six spirit lamps.
All this fuss over the littlest emperor.
All those desires bound and gagged.

IV

Dear Diary,
It's happened every night now for over two weeks.
They just won't leave. They complain of the food and the damp and
    the wretched view.

But as misery loves company, we stay on, a dusty motley,
packed and plucky like a sorority house during rush.
                       —Catastrophically yours, etc.
P.S.
The minor characters have been pushed out of bed.
They were told to wait on the balcony and not hope for too much.

V

Here comes the Slavic sandman in his fur cap—
the eternal one who in his bag of tricks
slings mud and spare ribs instead of sweet dreams.

VI

Sometimes I long for dear Anna K. in my bed:
at least she knew what she wanted,
at least she looked good in her dress.
If I threw myself in front of a subway train in tulle and crinoline
holding my reticule and wearing a little lace veil,
would any, any, anyone imagine
that I was her spitting image—that I was the modern Karenina?
that I died beautifully in one fell swoop—
or would I have to write and write and write that too?

Cul-de-sac

—in a subway in St. Petersburg, Russia

Four stops to Mayakovskaya
faces smudged with newspaper print
a fat man talks into his crumpled hands
everyone blinks their stares away from him
thick wind blows his hair up and out
there is no morning now
he mouths—
how did I get here?
the subway jerks to a halt,
doors thud open and—

Our Lady of the Russian Baths

In the Russian baths of Dostoyevskaya street
the grit of Nevsky Prospekt disappears
sweet in the steam—
scents from soaking eucalyptus and birch.

The motion back and forth of loofah and soap,
pumice and creams, honey and herbs—
women everywhere you look.

They stand around the room
as if on an ancient frieze
and continue their slow, ritual cleansing.

A woman rinses her feet and slowly turns to look at me.
She's wearing a gas mask—
features disfigured, myopic—
her breath is visible on the inside of the mask
and the haze in the room is like incense from a Mass.

Her head ticks back and forth like a pendulum,
it's some kind of requiem, a prayer she repeats—
Our Lady of Kazan,
Our Lady of the Sign,
Our Lady of the Don—
she murmurs—
Russia is a woman.

Rhapsody in Blue in Front of a Statue of Alexander Pushkin

—St. Petersburg, Russia

I

She works magic from the radius
of her Russian hips, pressing
blue thighs together, jeans grazing
the pavement—lusting
after Pushkin, pelvis to poet,
who from above demands with open palms
bread and butter, a pinch of salt, a breast—
something to cup in his oversized hands.

II

A bird perches on the poet's head,
women touch their hair on a further bench,
men smoke, read papers and roll cigarettes
and everyone seems to forget
the brash rhapsody in blue
with ferocious hips that rise and fall
in hopes of luring someone
into the trap of her looks.

III

Hours later, she's still there,
lingering and longing in the public square,
fencing thin fingers through long black hair
waiting for her own bronze horseman
or for any john to ride her away
from this midnight-blue fix
into the white nights of early morning.

The *Prix-fixe* in Petersburg

"Russia's vast range of climates and cultures has produced a diverse culinary repertoire."
—Catherine Philips, *St. Petersburg Dorling Kindersley Travel Guides*

Bar tid-bits, aperitivs and groseries,
frog paws under cognac sauce, chicken backed with cheese.

Beer having poured, dishes from a bird.
Bull testicles and fried sucking pig,
macaroni with crab meet.

Pickled mashrooms, garnishes, tea-pot,
paprika salad, solted nuts, coffee-cup.

Beef in the Old Russian stile under the apple sauce,
filet of duck with gentle fruit sauce,
with rosy souce, with soured cream,
with sauce 'pink juicy.'

Bouillon with chicken bowels,
gaspaccio with small crawfish tails.

Staffed chicken, sguids, greek fig-free,
Guail egg, shimps, groat cheese, kivi.

Salmon in wall nats, with rise and greens.
The three fats, cake of cottage cheese.

Favorite porridge of Peter the Great,
A duet of three pairs, Pfeffer stake.

Fruit and cream busket,
chicken lever and garlic rusk,
biled hot dog,
Sevenfoots,
blue job,
slow down,
pleasure up.

IV

Epilogue in a City Garden

An old couple, bent, the lady with a humpback, the man with a cane and a small hat, move barely across the way in front of me. I try to read. Looking up from the edge of my book, their shuffling feet chalk up white ground and raise cursive from the margin where I start up in my olive metal chair—indentions on my back and legs. Their narrow bodies like roman numerals.

How many chapters have they lived together? Enough to hump her back the shape of an "n" and he bent over into his cane pressing down on the earth pressing up against him, the letter "R." Back down again into my book, another paragraph, and the old woman trips against a small white stone, a comma, then the man steadies her with his crumpled hand, curved and rounded from so many cigarettes and breasts, curved with love and with life, it curves a "c" around her frail waist. Flowers fan behind them, a delicate wheel, folding out, in light colors, towards a sky of printed pages.

The Flying Machine, or Elegy for the Twentieth Century

"Between the lips and the voice something goes dying.
Something with the wings of a bird, something of anguish
   and oblivion."
                              —Pablo Neruda, "I Have Gone Marking"

I
It started centuries ago with da Vinci,
the architect in search of heights,
sketching flight with pencil and pen.

Time flies when it can.

Centuries later, out from the shadows comes modern man—
that flying machine with wings—
muscling in, solo, macho, chiaroscuro.

II
In his pinstripe three-piece suit, he flies over Paris
as high as Haussmann, over even Eiffel
with a souped-up *Renault 5 chevaux* strapped on his back
and sees that the world is not simply rose or empty blue—
that it is not a period, period.

III
From his perspective up in the gods, Paris is pointillist: the Opéra, the
Louvre, the Grand Palais. Constructivism on the Champs-Elysées.
He hovers over a Cubist merry-go-round, then, circling the cemetery
where Art Deco lies in a fresh mound, he spirals past Dada down into
Futurism, when the future was a manifesto signed by Italians, when one
letter of the alphabet was a poem and it made sense, when the future
had an *I* and when *I* was new, when Paris was ancient and the world had
no curfew. When women had little brown mice as pets and brought
them to the *café terrasse* on a leather leash. When a nude descending a
staircase decomposed crowds. When Nijinsky, the clown of God, hit
his head against the godless walls of Switzerland. The camera shot him
soaring, so proud to be the acrobat, Petrushka a dead doll, the specter

of his rose gone limp, just another twisted stem in God's funeral
garland.

IV

In the City, London gone brown and dun, he flies by Lloyds,
past T. S. Eliot smoking behind a banker's lamp—
a green pasted face staring with pursed lips
at the mirror in the lobby's distance.
The banker flinches as a bird sputters against a windowpane,
falls away towards the pavement,
then wings up and off to the left.
Ashes in an ashtray.

V

Now his wings are gone, and the gods have gone home
shut their doors, closed the shutters,
and the butchers and bakers have swept up,
now that some dictators have died
and flowers have been placed on their graves,
now that those flowers have faded in stone vases
and the water smells with that fowl green stink,
I come out to tell you that this, my friend, is how it is:

The dawn smell on a battlefield. Thick green and red.
That emerging from the mouth of the Métro
a man stumbles past bars and dance halls, cafés and kiosks,
checks his pocket watch—scraped fob silver plate—
and stumbles towards a dark room—it's getting late.

Le Bête humaine

Past the café in the train station, the kiosk selling daily news,
whores selling their daily wares, men smoking moist cigars,
a train speeds on as its whistle screams
in a rush to arrive in Paris.

With no time to slow down, no time for time,
the train skips the tracks,
a screech, some soot, a lost shoe—
black arabesques twist in a grimace—
the train slams through the station.

A bookstall is hit—papers fly up,
penny dreadfuls rip to shreds,
words and love letters tossed with black soot,
books' spines broken, dust covers covered with dust.

In the rush, the well-thumbed faces of passengers blur—
gravel lodged in groomed beards, splintering glass,
a child's broken wooden whistle, blood on a bustle.

With a plunge as clean as an exclamation point,
la bête humaine rams out of control,
nose first into macadam, deeper towards dirt,
desperately back into earth

while all the time, a woman looks on, touches her hair,
a small boy throws a ball against a stone wall,
and somewhere a farmer continues to plow his fields.

Broad Strokes in a Wine Bar

The woman wearing green shoes is drunk. She laughs in lurid light, red head against a yellow wall, an ancient Bardot. Her teeth have a look of soft charcoal, her tongue a blackened wafer. She pets on men to offer her one drink and then another. The soft undersides of her arms are stained with Burgundy and grey. She tells her life story like a painting by Chagall—a violinist upturns a table on the ceiling, white brides float down dark corridors and red horses run as she runs and runs away, her feet stained with deep green grass. She's the portrait of Paris in the Second World War, she's what's left of occupied France.

Pledge

I pledge allegiance, one under and indivisible,
under gorgeous eyes, my hand over my heart, bullets.

This is Vincent my sovereign state and victory by my side,
the boy who stomps and starts through his native *Marseillaise*—

the seduction of blood and vile,
slit throats of sons and friends—

aux armes, citoyens—with just his desk between us
march and march on—far away from this dangerous impasse.

I've just come to tutor you
in my native humble tongue

your eyes the color of the sky of Lille—
ssshhhhh—the shutters are closed.

Oh beautiful! O boy! Above the fruited plain,
I take dark bites from the corner of your lips with the corner of my eyes

and for a moment, and for amber waves of grain,
I feel that wicked twitch of *l'entre deux jambes*.

In the hush hush kingdom of your room,
all we need is a dictionary and some bottled water,

your lean lank, our anemone love.
All the little flags are flying in my heart.

Flagrant, you say, *invincible, sadistic, supremacy*—your words, not mine:
you've taken on my history.

Allons enfants de la Patrie, in this twin bed
thin enough for two under one cover, *mon enfant*,

we're as innocent as that faun in the afternoon.

Let me put my mother tongue into your vernacular,
bitter, sweeter—a little better,

o my vulgar vulgar.

And in between my God and the flag and the fifty-one states,
Betsy Ross and your upstart coltish tongue,

let me love you from this side of the desk,
and with my pen, let me guide your hand.

The Bibliothèque nationale
—Paris

In the Reading Room, all is hushed—
only beasts of books rage untamed.

The readers and researchers under the limpid light
of banker's lamps are colored absinthe green.

Their backs are shadowed black over dark pages.
In their hands are little blocks of god: books.

Soirée with Shark Suicide

Dear Odette,

It happened again—dinner died in my dressing room. Just when the guests were about to arrive, I went to put on Great Grandmother's string of pearls and *voilà*—my naughty entrée had had other plans!

No suicide note—not a bloody word—this is the second seafood suicide of the year—and in my boudoir no less. Was it the smell of my sauce? My lack of foresight for suitable seasonings?

O, darling, this does not bode well for my love life, no, not in the least. Whatever happens, we must keep this from Charles . . . it would ruin my chances, for sure . . . .

The nerve of that hulking fish, nubbing into family jewels, bloodying up my brooches, undermining my finely wrought plans!

How could I serve such a thing to my distinguished guests? They are so clever—for certain they would have suspected something—or, even worse—swallowed a stray pearl!

Of course I was forced to abandon the entire evening—dashed off notes that I was terribly indisposed—

This is the last time that any seafood makes a funeral wake out of one of my soirées—I will only serve fowl from now on, and the finest, so there!

What *is* a girl to do? It's a Chanel funeral posy in my dressing room, darling!

Mournfully yours—

The Seventh Art in the Sanatorium

"Louis Lumière was on the board of directors of a sanatorium near Lyon and most likely donated films including "Heavy Weather on the Sea, No. 2" to the institution to show patients."

—news dispatch from French Consulate

I Turn of a Century

When menstruation was alarming and Mesmer all the rage,

when hysterical women were locked away—

forced flowers in a hothouse, *les fleurs du mal*—

when one was sane or insane with nothing

in between but a doctor's *pince-nez,*

the Lumière brothers, gods of the seventh art,

sat on the board of a sanatorium and made decisions about madness.

II Heavy Weather on the Sea, No. 2

As the sea swells on a painted screen,

patients sit in the false night

and remember their lives by and by—

the stream by the path, the sea at large.

Metal chairs scrape, the room grows hot.

Clouds move in with thunder and rain. Lightning in eyes.

They could easily drown in thought.

This film breaks hearts back to where they were once—

the afternoon spent on a boat,

the picnic in the park, the feel of rain on bare arms,

the earth soft under foot and flowers and frost—

to the slap in the face, the rape, the grainy visage behind a veil.

III Piano, pianoforte

And the noise is unbearable, though there is little sound,
though the player piano plays on
and begins its stilted jag again and again,
with a tinny ringing in the ears,
out of tune, in the back of the room,
the rolled pages turn over and over again.

IV Envoi

Picture a small opening in the heart—
a valve, a vent, that lets light in—
for now and then,
life is not a foreign element to them.

V

Rapunzel on an Ironing Board

—for Carol Jean and Mary Jean

My mother and grandmother stand over the porcelain sink
with its long silver snout where water too hot or cold
streams out and onto my aching scalp.

The three of us are in the kitchen: red Formica, white sink, metal
    ironing board.
Dark clouds of copper pots hover above my head.
Flat out on the board, my feet reach halfway to the end.

I take tight hold and grit my teeth and count:
one, two, three, four, knots, nails, snarls, ouch—
yes it's almost over yes it will end yes it will stop and not begin again

and then they'll wrap my damp hair in a big blue towel
and I'll be the queen of Sheba in my robe for an hour.

And they will smooth my hair over my shoulders
and braid little secrets into dark meshes
and I will have three guesses to guess their wishes.

And now, touching the crown of my head
or pulling back black loose strands
in the thick of my roots I still feel
the faint, leftover sting of their hands.

In a Train Tunnel

I

The rails crack once, your only warning—
in that sigh rests your life.
you start toward the distant light, pinhole size—
a tickle in your throat.

II

Running now, your mind lags behind your feet—
soot falls forward—
and racing, racing light grows by leaps.

III

Rushing out of the tunnel, breathless
into brash light, turned back
from the childhood you left at the other end,
your hair blows up and out
and against your face is the *whoosh* of a thousand nails,
black metal sky.

IV

Earth shaking, body trembling—
not from fear—there was no time—
the quake comes from your organs—
your physical jargon exposed—
bile in your mouth, gullet in your throat.
Your body has arrived before you.

V

And just as it came, the train is gone again,
the whistle only now warning you of something long past:
the train at its breakneck pace,
the wheels reciting *it's too late, too late.*

Director of the Feast

I

The god of good luck is winking at you. Dimples in his hairy ass. He sees that spring in your step. Yes, that's shrimp sauce on his tux—on the white part, underneath his chin. He's got a fork in his pocket, a wooden nickel under his tongue, and boy is he happy to see you. The censor between your legs is warming up. Hang on Sloopy. He tells you he likes to be spanked (for some kind of shock effect) but you couldn't care less. *Keep the champagne flowing!* you say, even though this is something you never say.

II

Now he's feeding you Swedish meatballs with a toothpick. He says, *Hubba hubba—you are dressed to the nines!* And what he says is not a lie. Not at all.

III

Though smorgasbords aren't really your thing, here you are, standing in line again. Your friend's gone over to attack the cash bar. *Kill two birds with one stone, you know. . . .* That's what you hear yourself saying. *O, but it takes two*, he answers, sphinx-like, though he doesn't look anything like a sphinx.

IV

Sidling up with two martinis he says, *Les jeux sont faits. Rien ne va plus.* Now well into the swing of things, you swagger back, *Shaken, not stirred?*, and think what a shoddy 007 you would make and that this is no way to impress your buddy who looks a little bit like Sacha Guitry around the ears and then he looks at you straight in the eyes just like your grandmother used to and he points his pointer finger at you just like your grandmother used to (which isn't easy because he's still holding two martinis) and says, *Chérie, mon amie, ma petite, mon âme soeur, ma toute belle—rien ne va plus.*

V

Behind you, someone's whining about the last days of Pompeii. A reception line forms on the other side of the ballroom. *Just what kind of costume party is this, anyway?* you ask him.

Envoi

It all depends, he grins. Yuck yuck. You guessed right: Lucifer. Jump in.

Découpage and the Dark Experiment

"Not everyone is sensitive to 'the thing.' 'The thing' doesn't recognize
itself unless it is madness or genius."
                              —Marie Cardinal, *The Words to Say It*

I
Here I sit in the blue room with its chagrin,
practicing Italian, folding laundry. It's 10:30 p.m.
Per favore. Dov'è la stazione ferroviaria. Et cetera.
Upstairs a phone is ringing. The dog is panting.
Doors open and close. Someone sobs.
A stifled voice. *A destra.* Right. Right.

II
I have to wear this scarf on my head—it protects me from them.
This is my painting this is not my painting.
I'm pregnant. I need some cocaine. How are you? Fine, fine.
I walk to keep the voices away. Do you see
that angel? He's been here all day crouching
with his skirt around his knees, showing
his crotch to the bees. What are those video cameras?
Why? What are they trying to see? Why
are you taping me? I thought that clock was a camera.
That's my painting, yes.
Fine. I don't want to go to the hospital.
Don't. Where are we going? Where?

III
A toothpick stuck in an apple core.
Sawdust sprinkled on a sidewalk.
Coffee grounds mounded on the bathroom floor.
Cut and paste. The découpage of an entire life in one afternoon.

IV
It's not amnesia. It's not exactly dementia. A *fata morgana.*
Perhaps something else—passing psychosis,

Drugs or some dark experiment.
Schizophrenia? I didn't say it—that was someone else.

V

Upstairs, with her audience of one,
she sits hard as stone
and hugs herself into oblivion.
She spirals toward babble,
one verb in a crowd of nouns,
a run-on sentence that ends
abruptly, unexpectedly.

VI

She grins at the ceiling
as a huge camera lens
with a tiny eye shoots all of her selves.
She offers all up to the gods
just this once
then in a wink, she's gone.

VII

The phones are ringing for angry ghosts
and the girl with no name—
she doesn't even own her face.

For Death and the Maiden

I
My grandmother bent over her bath,
flesh sagging, belly bloated, hanging—
her back soft,
strangely beautiful
as before.

II
A scar the length of an arm
from fingertip to shoulder,
straight as the letter *l*,
tender as a baby's eyelid purple and veined.

III
There is no *I* in death.
No vowel sound.
Just a pause between
the open casket and the dirt mound.

IV
The "o" in phone, in the empty room,
the open mouth, the dry throat.
Of calling out and no voice,
now, or ever again.

V
For what we wait for
this fall, no, this winter,
no, spring, snow
in May, no spring,
summer—while I'm away
in Saint Petersburg with its white nights
that do not sleep.

Epithalamium
—for D. and M.

In that photograph you sent, the one with flowers behind,

I could tell you their color but not what they were,

I could count the times we've spoken on the phone,

the color of the Danish man's eyes.

It's him, you, in that photograph with the flowers.

But that was weeks ago—years.

I think that's what you said, 'It's in his eyes.'

When we spoke it was the day after your wedding and you and I were
far away.

It's in your hands, like everything else.

I could tell you that Istanbul was built on seven hills, that Copenhagen
has four syllables,

that there will be happiness and more.

But why—

just look up.

Postcard Home
—*Istanbul*

The hotel room's an absolute disaster. Your feet under your head, etc. The Turkish dwarf, *il tappo*, that terrible Turkish plug, squats downstairs and hands you a dirty key when you come in. His moustache a miniature Sadaam—name's Mutate or Mugwump. (Told me Murat but I don't believe him.) Two black cats on the front step—the only good luck. Just look at the ruin here. "Magnificent decay, etc." Wish you were here.

Postscript by a Park Bench

Every time I leave this garden,
my shoes are covered with fine white powder,
a beautiful dirt, so that when I go home,
dusty and out of sorts, slouched,
I dream I've written all over the city in these black boots.
(At night I like to clean them—
to erase my mistakes.)

Sweet Woodruff

Slowly it grew back, that gift of sweet
Woodruff. Thank God—thought I'd killed it off—almost
Everything last month seemed to wither in the heat—
Even me—roots choked in baked earth. Yet the most
Terrifying thing: how indifferent I
Was. That Indian summer gift singed, no wood
Or sweet left, just burnt bark, November dry,
Overlooked, underfed. Then he said I could
Do it: cut out the dead parts. Perhaps I cut down to
Roots, almost, unbelieving. See, I've killed all
Of my plants. It's a bad habit I have,
Unintentional, yet quite revealing: a true
Green thumb. But your sweet woodruff proved this fall
How roots survive, even as leaves starve.

Elegy in India Ink

"Le suicide offre tous les avantages: c'est raffiné, c'est chargé de sens, c'est fin-de-siècle."
"Suicide offers every advantage: it's refined, it's filled with meaning, it's fin-de-siècle."

—Tonino Benaquista, *Saga*

I
Before the traffic of human lives made headlines,
(opening inside page of a Monday *New York Times*),
four virgins of the village of Bhilai,
inland from the Bay of Bengal,
not far from Bangladesh or Nepal, in India,
on the seventh of April, sisters,
committed suicide.

Aged sixteen to twenty-four,
Minakshi, Meena, Hemlata, and Kesar
wrote a note on lined paper that they left near the door:
We four sisters are fed up with our lives.

They started early the night before.
They pooled their money and bought some cakes.
They stayed up late playing card games and tricks.
They played with words.
They stayed awake.
They ate sweets until they were sick.
They fell asleep on the concrete floor.
One, two, three, four:
the early hours quickly passed.
One, two, three, four:
they hung themselves from rafters with long scarves.

II
The calligraphy of bodies in mid-air,
dim in the dusty light,
spelled out the sisters' last wish.

Something still lived in those dark silhouettes,
in the alphabet of limbs and in the stiff grey lips,
something desperate and deliberate,
impossible for the illiterate,
something illegible, difficult at first, faint,
then, on second glance, was quite clear
and impossible to erase:
Minakshi, Meena, Hemlata, Kesar.
It was their names, their names that lived there.

III

In the West, suicide is linked to mental illness—depression, dementia,
    suicidal tendencies.
Schizophrenia, neurasthenia, panic disorders, the willies.
In the West, suicide is all in the head.

In the East, they say that suicide is perhaps a different malaise—social,
    economic, political.
A question of caste, of debt, of ancestry, of industry.
One of arranged marriages, dowries, *paneer*, chutney, education,
    elephants, offspring.
Of sacred cows with six legs, of an ancient society in a new century.
Of something else, something indistinct and obscure:
the shadows of so many women and their weight in the third world.

IV

Perhaps our word *suicide* contains an answer to their death:
s, a thinly curved consonant escaping into air,
u, the you, the incriminating vowel,
the twins, *i*, that cancel one another out,
cancel out the self,
the sluice and wave of *c*,
d, soft thud of tongue against gums, penultimate
before the demise, the *coup de grace*, mum—
the final, silent *e*.
But this is all Occidental.
Their suicide was premeditated, Oriental.

74

V
On the palms of their hands,
on the soles of their feet,
on the walls of their house,
they wrote their names.
Blue ink stained deep
skin, smooth and pale as parchment,
marked walls discolored with dirt,
and in few words spelled out their suicide note,
their final, desperate hope:
Minakshi, Meena, Hemlata, Kesar.

Recent Titles in the Carnegie Mellon Poetry Series

2000
Small Boat with Oars of Different Size, Thom Ward
Post Meridian, Mary Ruefle
Hierarchies of Rue, Roger Sauls
Constant Longing, Dennis Sampson
Mortal Education, Joyce Peseroff
How Things Are, James Richardson
Years Later, Gregory Djanikian
On the Waterbed They Sank to Their Own Levels, Sarah Rosenblatt
Blue Jesus, Jim Daniels
Winter Morning Walks: 100 Postcards to Jim Harrison, Ted Kooser

2001
The Deepest Part of the River, Mekeel McBride
The Origin of Green, T. Alan Broughton
Day Moon, Jon Anderson
Glacier Wine, Maura Stanton
Earthly, Michael McFee
Lovers in the Used World, Gillian Conoley
Sex Lives of the Poor and Obscure, David Schloss
Voyages in English, Dara Wier
Quarters, James Harms
Mastodon, 80% Complete, Jonathan Johnson
Ten Thousand Good Mornings, James Reiss
The World's Last Night, Margot Schilpp

2002
Among the Musk Ox People, Mary Ruefle
What it Wasn't, Laura Kasischke
The Finger Bone, Kevin Prufer
The Late World, Arthur Smith
Slow Risen Among the Smoke Trees, Elizabeth Kirschner
Keeping Time, Suzanne Cleary
Astronaut, Brian Henry

2003
Imitation of Life, Allison Joseph
A Place Made of Starlight, Peter Cooley
The Mastery Impulse, Ricardo Pau-Llosa
Except for One Obscene Brushstroke, Dzvinia Orlowsky
Taking Down the Angel, Jeff Friedman
Casino of the Sun, Jerry Williams
Trouble, Mary Baine Campbell
Lives of Water, John Hoppenthaler

2004
Freeways and Aqueducts, James Harms
Tristimania, Mary Ruefle
Prague Winter, Richard Katrovas
Venus Examines Her Breast, Maureen Seaton
Trains in Winter, Jay Meek
The Women Who Loved Elvis All Their Lives,
        Fleda Brown
The Chronic Liar Buys a Canary, Elizabeth Edwards
Various Orbits, Thom Ward

2005
Laws of My Nature, Margot Schilpp
Things I Can't Tell You, Michael Dennis Browne
Renovation, Jeffrey Thomson
Sleeping Woman, Herbert Scott
Blindsight, Carol Hamilton
Fallen from a Chariot, Kevin Prufer
Needlegrass, Dennis Sampson
Bent to the Earth, Blas Manuel De Luna

2006
Burn the Field, Amy Beeder
Dog Star Delicatessen: New and Selected Poems 1979–2006,
        Mekeel McBride
The Sadness of Others, Hayan Charara
A Grammar to Waking, Nancy Eimers
Shinemaster, Michael McFee
Eastern Mountain Time, Joyce Peseroff
Dragging the Lake, Robert Thomas

2007
So I Will Till the Ground, Gregory Djanikian
Trick Pear, Suzanne Cleary
Indeed I Was Pleased With the World, Mary Ruefle
The Situation, John Skoyles
One Season Behind, Sarah Rosenblatt
The Playhouse Near Dark, Elizabeth Holmes
Drift and Pulse, Kathleen Halme
Black Threads, Jeff Friedman
On the Vanishing of Large Creatures, Susan Hutton

2008
The Grace of Necessity, Samuel Green
After West, James Harms
The Book of Sleep, Eleanor Stanford
Anticipate the Coming Reservoir, John Hoppenthaler
Parable Hunter, Ricardo Pau-Llosa
Convertible Night, Flurry of Stones, Dzvinia Orlowsky

2009
Divine Margins, Peter Cooley
Cultural Studies, Kevin A. Gonzalez
Cave of the Yellow Volkswagen, Maureen Seaton
Group Portrait from Hell, David Schloss
Birdwatching in Wartime, Jeffrey Thomson
Dear Apocalypse, K. A. Hays
Warhol-o-rama, Peter Oresick

2010
Admission, Jerry Williams
The Other Life: Selected Poems, Herbert Scott
In the Land We Imagined Ourselves, Jonathan Johnson
The Diminishing House, Nicky Beer
Selected Early Poems: 1958-1983, Greg Kuzma
Say Sand, Daniel Coudriet
A World Remembered, T. Alan Broughton
Knock Knock, Heather Hartley